For Maxine

tiger tales
an imprint of ME Media, LLC
202 Old Ridgefield Road, Wilton, CT 06897
Published in the United States 2006
Originally published in Great Britain 2006
By Little Tiger Press
An imprint of Magi Publications
Text and illustration copyright ©2006 Matt Buckingham
CIP data is available
ISBN-13: 978-1-58925-059-8
ISBN-10: 1-58925-059-1
Printed in China

Bright Stanley

by Matt Buckingham

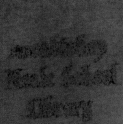

tiger tales

Far below the waves, a little fish named Stanley lived with his school. They were the brightest, sparkliest fish of the deep, dark sea.

One morning, Stanley woke up late.
"Hellooo! It's me-e!" he called to his friends.
But the reef was strangely quiet.

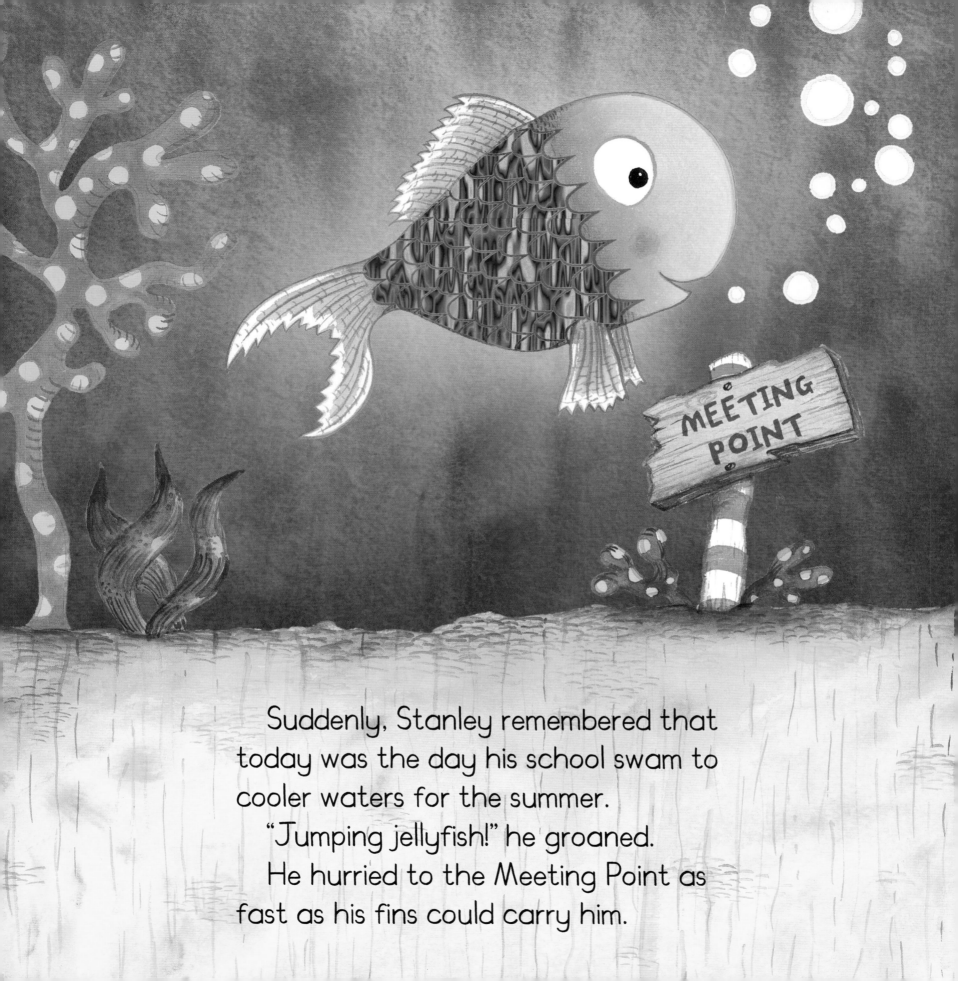

Suddenly, Stanley remembered that today was the day his school swam to cooler waters for the summer.

"Jumping jellyfish!" he groaned.

He hurried to the Meeting Point as fast as his fins could carry him.

But no one was there.
As he looked around, he saw
a bright light.
"Aha! They haven't gone far,"
he said, and he raced toward
the glow.

But it was only a lobster counting coins.
"Go away! Don't touch my treasure," the
lobster growled, snip-snapping his claws.
"I'm looking for my friends," said Stanley.

"Fish," the lobster grumbled. "Those others were in such a hurry to find someone they upset my coins."

"Others?" asked Stanley. "My friends!"

"Join them then," snarled the lobster, and Stanley sped off.

Ahead of him, Stanley saw a shimmer. He could just make out a bright, sparkly fish. One of his friends!

"Hellooo! It's me-e!" he called, swimming faster.

CLONK!

Stanley crashed headfirst into something hard.

"Jumping jellyfish!" he cried. It wasn't one of his friends at all, but his own reflection in a shiny pearl!

Stanley rubbed his bumped nose,
feeling a little dazed. He didn't notice
the dark shape coming up behind him.

When he turned around, Stanley found himself staring straight into the mouth of a huge...

"Aaaaa!" Stanley shrieked. Over coral and under weeds he sped with the shark snapping at his tail.

Finally, Stanley saw a small hole in a rock below. He dived down inside to just miss being gobbled up!

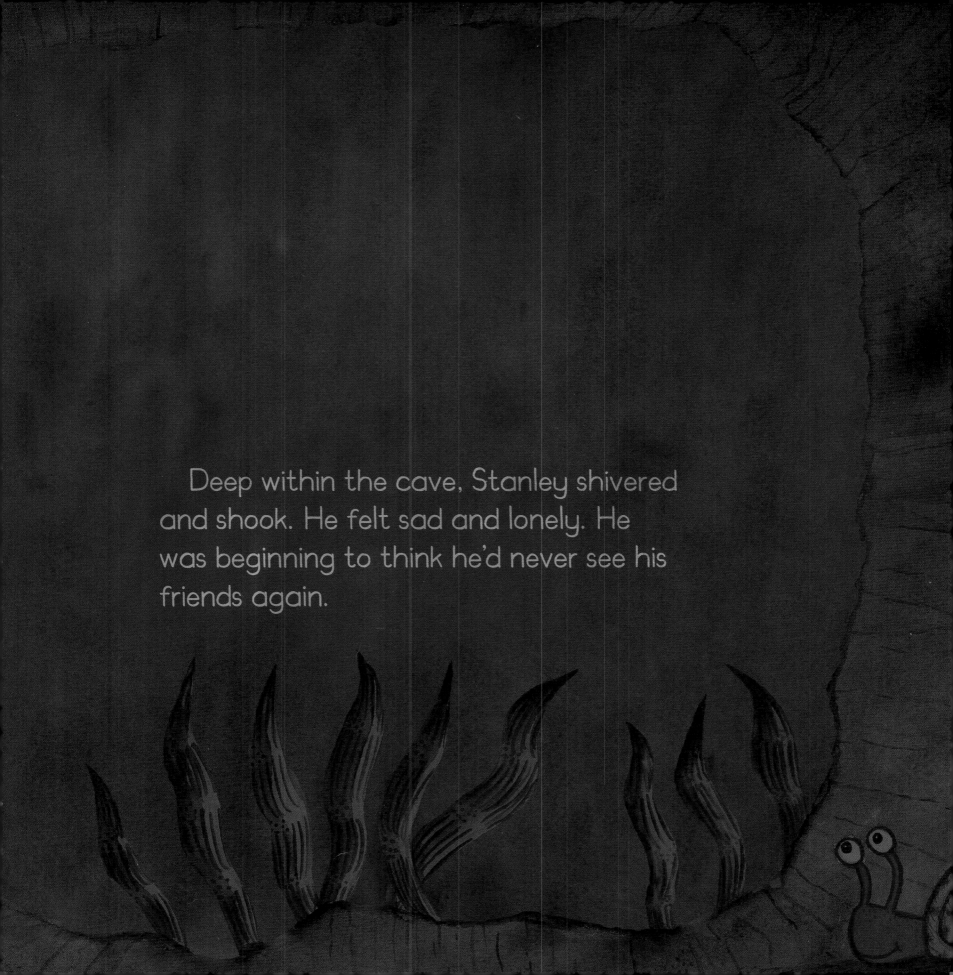

Deep within the cave, Stanley shivered and shook. He felt sad and lonely. He was beginning to think he'd never see his friends again.

"Well, I can't stay here forever," he said at last. Stanley poked his head out of the cave to see if the shark had left.

"Jumping jellyfish!" he squealed.

The sea was a golden orange, glowing and glittering. It was the most wonderful sight he had ever seen because there, in front of him, were . . .

his friends!

"Hellooo! It's me-e!" he called.

"Stanley!" his friends cheered. "Where have you been? We've been looking all over for you!"

And Stanley told them his adventures as they swam off in one bright, sparkly, happy school.